D1276858

First Ladies

Nancy Reagan

Joanne Mattern

ABDO
Publishing Company

visit us at
www.abdopublishing.com

Published by ABDO Publishing Company, 8000 West 78th Street, Edina, Minnesota 55439.
Copyright © 2008 by Abdo Consulting Group, Inc. International copyrights reserved in all
countries. No part of this book may be reproduced in any form without written permission from the
publisher. The Checkerboard Library™ is a trademark and logo of ABDO Publishing Company.

Printed in the United States.

Cover Photo: Courtesy Ronald Reagan Presidential Library
Interior Photos: AP Images pp. 11, 13, 31; Corbis pp. 22, 27; Getty Images pp. 12, 15; Courtesy
    Ronald Reagan Presidential Library pp. 5, 6, 7, 8, 9, 10, 11, 16, 17, 18, 19, 20, 21, 23, 24, 25;
    U.S. Navy p. 26

Series Coordinator: BreAnn Rumsch
Editors: Rochelle Baltzer, BreAnn Rumsch
Art Direction & Cover Design: Neil Klinepier

Library of Congress Cataloging-in-Publication Data

Mattern, Joanne, 1963-
  Nancy Reagan / Joanne Mattern.
    p. cm. -- (First ladies)
  Includes index.
  ISBN-13: 978-1-59928-799-7
  1. Reagan, Nancy, 1923---Juvenile literature. 2. Presidents' spouses--United States--Biography--
Juvenile literature. 3. Reagan, Ronald--Juvenile literature. I. Title.
  E878.R43.M37 2008
  973.927092--dc22
  [B]
                                                                    2007009734

Contents

Nancy Reagan

Nancy Reagan was First Lady of the United States between 1981 and 1989. She was married to Ronald Reagan, the country's fortieth president.

At first, some people did not like Mrs. Reagan. They felt that she did not understand regular Americans. However during her time as First Lady, she worked hard to change that impression. Mrs. Reagan took part in various programs and events that helped many people.

Mrs. Reagan felt honored to be First Lady. But the most important thing in her life was her family. Mr. and Mrs. Reagan had an especially strong bond. In fact, their marriage remains one of America's greatest love stories.

Nancy Reagan overcame much criticism to become a well-loved First Lady.

Born into Theater

Anne Frances Robbins was born in New York City, New York, on July 6, 1921. Everyone called the little girl Nancy. Her parents were Edith Luckett Robbins and Kenneth Robbins. Unfortunately, Edith and Kenneth divorced soon after Nancy was born.

Nancy stayed with Edith, who performed in plays throughout the country. Nancy thought the theater was a fun place to be. For the next few years, Nancy spent a lot of time backstage with her mother. "I loved to dress up in her stage clothes, put on her makeup, and pretend that I was playing her part," Nancy later wrote.

However, Edith did not think the theater was a good place to raise a child. She wanted her daughter to have a more normal life. So, she sent Nancy to live with her aunt, uncle, and cousin. Nancy lived with them in Bethesda, Maryland, for several years.

Nancy had a happy childhood with her aunt and uncle. However, her fondest memories are of her mother's visits.

As a young girl, Nancy loved having tea parties with her dolls.

A New Father

When Nancy was eight years old, her mother remarried. Edith's new husband, Loyal Davis, was a doctor in Chicago, Illinois. Edith and Nancy moved there to live with him.

Loyal was a well-known **neurosurgeon**. Nancy enjoyed going to the hospital with him to watch him work. Loyal's job made him wealthy. So for the first time, Nancy led a privileged life. She received a private education at Girls' Latin School. Her favorite subject there was drama.

Loyal was a kind man. Nancy grew to love her stepfather very much. He loved Nancy too, and

Loyal did his best to make Nancy (left) happy. This included arranging special visits with her cousin Charlotte (right).

he treated her like his own daughter. When Nancy was 14 years old, Loyal adopted her. From then on, she was known as Nancy Davis.

Nancy graduated from Girls' Latin School in 1939. Then, she attended Smith College in Northampton, Massachusetts. At that time, Smith was an all-girls school. It was also one of the most renowned schools in the country. Nancy enjoyed her years at the college. There, she studied English and theater. Nancy dreamed of being an actress, just like her mother.

Nancy loved acting in plays during college. In 1943, she starred in The Glamour Girl.

Chasing Dreams

Nancy graduated from Smith College in 1943. At that time, the United States was fighting in **World War II**. So, she returned to Chicago to work in a hospital. Many of Nancy's patients were injured soldiers who had fought in the war.

Nancy's publicity portraits helped her find work as an actress.

Still, Nancy didn't give up her dream of becoming an actress. She wanted to be onstage entertaining people. Luckily, Nancy's mother was friends with Zasu Pitts, a famous actress. In 1945, Pitts offered Nancy a part in a Broadway show called *Ramshackle Inn*. Nancy happily said yes! She moved to New York City to begin a new life.

Nancy's first Broadway part was very small. She only had three lines. However, she had more lines in her second Broadway show, *Lute Song*. Nancy acted in several other plays in New York after that. She also appeared on some television shows. However, she still dreamed of bigger and better things.

In 1949, Nancy moved to Los Angeles, California, to pursue a film career in Hollywood. That year, she **auditioned** for MGM Studios. MGM signed her to a seven-year contract, and she went on to make 11 movies. Nancy loved being an actress! But she still had one more dream. She wanted to fall in love, get married, and have a family.

Nancy thought Hollywood was an exciting place to be. She worked with many famous actors and actresses from the 1950s.

Mrs. Ronald Reagan

Not long after joining MGM, Nancy met an actor named Ronald Reagan. He was tall, athletic, and handsome. Ronald had once been married to an actress named Jane Wyman. And, he already had two children, Maureen and Michael.

The Reagans enjoyed a quick, private wedding. In fact, they only invited two guests!

Soon, Ronald and Nancy fell in love. On March 4, 1952, they were married in Los Angeles. Later that year, the couple welcomed their new baby, Patricia Ann. They called her Patti. Nancy also cared for Maureen and Michael when they visited their father.

To help support her family, Nancy continued acting. In 1957, she and Ronald even appeared in a movie together. However, Nancy felt that her career kept her from spending enough time at home.

On May 20, 1958, Nancy and Ronald's second child arrived. They named the boy Ronald Prescott after his father. Then, Nancy gave up her career to stay home full-time. Her dream of having a family had come true!

On movie sets, Nancy and Ronald practiced their lines before filming. The two enjoyed working together.

California Politics

Mr. Reagan was a successful actor, but he was also interested in politics. During the 1960s, he gave up acting to pursue a political career. In 1966, Mr. Reagan was elected governor of California.

The family soon moved into the governor's mansion in Sacramento, California. However, Mrs. Reagan was horrified at the house's condition. The fire department even declared the building unsafe to live in. Mrs. Reagan was concerned for her family's safety.

The Reagans quickly moved out of the mansion and settled into a nice house nearby. Some people thought Mrs. Reagan was snobby for doing this. But, she believed caring for her family was more important than other people's opinions of her.

During this time, America was involved in the **Vietnam War**. Mrs. Reagan visited many of the wounded soldiers who had fought in the war. She also searched for information about U.S. soldiers who were missing in Vietnam

Mrs. Reagan wanted to help needy children and the elderly, too. In 1970, she began supporting the Foster Grandparent Program. This program pairs senior citizens with children who need adult guidance.

The Reagans posed for a campaign photo with their son, Ron.

To the White House

The Reagans enjoyed meeting their many supporters during the campaign.

Mr. Reagan was California's governor until 1975. Then, he decided to run for president. However, President Gerald Ford was nominated instead. In 1980, Mr. Reagan ran again and won the nomination. That November, he was elected the fortieth president of the United States!

In 1981, the Reagan family moved to Washington, D.C. There, Mrs. Reagan was surprised and upset by the White House's appearance. The building had become shabby over the past 20 years. The First Lady was determined to make the White House beautiful again. Over the next few months, many parts of the building were

repaired. Also, important pieces of furniture and art were removed from storage and displayed.

Private citizens paid for most of the White House repairs. Yet, some people were angry that Mrs. Reagan had asked for money to fix the building. At that time, America was in a serious **recession**. So, many Americans felt the money should have been used to help those in need. Once again, Mrs. Reagan was called a snob. Despite this disapproval, she did what she felt was right.

Mrs. Reagan was proud of her work on the White House's appearance. She especially enjoyed redecorating the Red Room.

Danger!

In March 1981, a man named John Hinkley tried to **assassinate** President Reagan. Hinkley shot the president in the chest. President Reagan was rushed to a hospital and underwent surgery to remove the bullet.

Mrs. Reagan loved her husband very much and was afraid he would die. Fortunately, he recovered quickly. When Mr. Reagan first saw his wife at the hospital, he told her, "Honey, I forgot to duck."

The assassination attempt made Mrs. Reagan worry about the president's safety. She even

Mrs. Reagan stayed by her husband's side during his recovery at George Washington University Hospital in Washington, D.C.

Mrs. Reagan enjoyed planning the fancy White House parties she and the president hosted.

talked to **astrologers**. She hoped they could tell her the best way to keep her husband out of danger.

When the public heard about the astrologers, some people laughed at the First Lady. They didn't understand how frightened she was. Mrs. Reagan was criticized for many other things, too. She wore fancy clothes and hosted expensive parties. This upset Americans who faced losing their jobs because of the **recession**. They felt the First Lady did not understand their lives.

"Just Say No"

The First Lady did not want to ignore people who needed help. She continued to support the Foster Grandparent Program. She also wanted to help children stay away from drugs. So in 1981, Mrs. Reagan began a program to educate children about the dangers of drug use.

The First Lady worked hard to get her message to as many young people as possible. She appeared on television, wrote articles, and visited drug treatment programs. She told young people that if anyone offered them drugs, they should "just say no."

In 1985, Mrs. Reagan extended her "Just Say No" drug campaign. She invited First Ladies from other countries to a special meeting in Washington, D.C. For two days, the world's most influential women talked about how to keep children off drugs.

Mrs. Reagan traveled to 65 cities in 33 states to warn children about the dangers of using drugs.

Still, some people thought that "Just Say No" was too simple. They didn't think it would keep kids from using drugs. However, many others appreciated the First Lady's efforts to raise drug awareness. Her campaign became famous.

U.S.A.

A Worthy Cause

Mrs. Reagan's efforts toward America's drug problem began with a simple phrase. She shared this approach with students across the country. But soon, it became evident that "Just Say No" wasn't enough.

The First Lady knew the drug problem extended beyond the United States. So, she made a point of traveling around the world and educating as many people as possible. In total, she traveled almost 250,000 miles (402,000 km). Then in 1988, Mrs. Reagan made history. She became the first American First Lady to speak to the United Nations General Assembly. She spoke about the need for drug education.

Additionally, the U.S. Department of Health and Human Services works to identify patterns of drug use and other issues facing Americans. To accomplish this, many surveys are conducted each year. In 1996, the Monitoring the Future Study reported that 40 percent of students had used drugs in 1979. However, this number had fallen to only 14 percent by 1992.

Despite early criticism, the First Lady's plan to prevent drug use has proven to be a success. The survey results indicate that the "Just Say No" campaign was an important first step in drug education. Today, many programs worldwide work against the drug problem. It seems that "Just Say No" was the beginning of a good thing.

Climb to the Top

The late 1980s proved challenging for the Reagans. Mrs. Reagan had not always gotten along with her daughter, Patti. In 1986, Patti wrote a novel about her family. The story made the First Lady seem like a mother who cared more about social position than her own family. Mr. and Mrs. Reagan were deeply hurt. They rarely spoke to Patti for many years after that.

In 1987, Mrs. Reagan found out she had **breast cancer**. She needed an operation to stop the disease. Fortunately, the First

Despite the challenges in her own life, Mrs. Reagan never stopped helping others. She continued to work with her antidrug campaign and the Foster Grandparent Program.

Lady made a complete recovery. Afterward, she wanted to raise awareness of the disease and how to treat it. She hoped to help other women prevent the illness.

Mrs. Reagan also had many happy moments during the 1980s. For several years, the American people ranked her as the most admired woman in the world! Mrs. Reagan also enjoyed working with her husband in the White House. Members of their staff later said that the president and First Lady made a good team. No one could get between their love for each other.

President and Mrs. Reagan give a joint radio address from Camp David, Maryland, the presidential retreat. Camp David was established in 1942 as a place for the president to relax and entertain.

A Long Good-bye

Mr. Reagan finished his presidency in January 1989. He and Mrs. Reagan returned to their ranch in California. They were looking forward to a long and happy retirement.

To continue her drug education program, Mrs. Reagan started the Nancy Reagan Foundation. This organization aided other drug-free programs. In 1991, she and her husband also opened the Ronald Reagan Presidential Library in Simi Valley, California. Many of Mr. Reagan's presidential papers are stored there.

The Reagans loved spending time on their mountaintop ranch, Rancho del Cielo. There, they rode horses and canoed on Lucky Lake.

But soon, Mrs. Reagan noticed that something was wrong with her husband. He forgot things and had trouble doing simple tasks. In 1994, the couple learned Mr. Reagan had **Alzheimer's disease**. Over time, he would forget almost everything and everyone he knew. Yet, he trusted his wife would stay beside him and they would face the disease together.

For the next ten years, Mrs. Reagan rarely left her husband's side. Sometimes she went out to lunch, but she was always eager to get home. In those years, the Reagan family surrounded Mr. Reagan with love and care. Mrs. Reagan's stepdaughter, Maureen, stayed close by. Even Patti connected with her parents again.

The Reagan family often went their separate ways.
However, Mr. and Mrs. Reagan were always happy to see
their children when they came home to visit.

Looking Ahead

On June 5, 2004, Ronald Reagan died at home in California. He was 93 years old. At the time of his death, he had lived longer than any other American president. Mr. Reagan was honored with a state funeral in Washington, D.C. Thousands of people attended the funeral and paid their respects. Mr. Reagan was remembered as a great president who made Americans proud again.

After her husband died, Mrs. Reagan kept his memory alive. And, she worked to inform Americans about medical experiments and treatments that might cure **Alzheimer's disease**. Mrs. Reagan hoped her painful experience could help others in the future.

Mrs. Reagan was often criticized for her actions while she was First Lady. But no matter what, she always carried herself gracefully. She worked to make a positive

Mrs. Reagan dedicated the USS Ronald Reagan, a navy aircraft carrier, on March 4, 2001.

impact during her years in the White House. So, she will be remembered as a great First Lady. But more than anything, Nancy Reagan was a true partner to her husband.

Today, Mrs. Reagan speaks about the ways science can benefit medicine.

Mrs. Reagan's Campaign

For the past several years, scientists have been researching the effects of stem cells. Unlike most cells, stem cells can become any type of tissue in the human body. They can be used to help many different illnesses and injuries. This makes stem cells very valuable to doctors and patients.

Some diseases, such as Alzheimer's disease, diabetes, and Parkinson's disease, do not yet have a cure. But, stem cells could someday change that. They might even help people with spinal cord injuries walk again!

For these reasons, many people strongly support stem cell research. Mrs. Reagan is an active supporter of this research, too. She is working to help scientists gain funding for their work. Mrs. Reagan has given many speeches throughout the country. She has also written letters to politicians regarding this research.

For her efforts, Scientific American magazine named Mrs. Reagan a leader in medical treatment policy in 2004. That year, she also received an award from the Juvenile Diabetes Research Foundation.

Timeline

1921	Anne Frances "Nancy" Robbins was born on July 6.
1939	Nancy graduated from Girls' Latin School.
1939–1943	Nancy attended Smith College.
1945	Nancy took her first professional acting role in *Ramshackle Inn*.
1952	Nancy married Ronald Reagan on March 4; their daughter, Patricia Ann, was born later that year.
1958	The Reagans' son, Ronald Prescott, was born.
1966–1975	Mr. Reagan served as governor of California.
1970	Mrs. Reagan began her work with the Foster Grandparent Program.
1981–1989	Mrs. Reagan acted as First Lady, while her husband served as president.
1981	President Reagan was shot in an assassination attempt; Mrs. Reagan began the "Just Say No" antidrug campaign.
1985	Mrs. Reagan invited First Ladies from around the world to Washington, D.C., to discuss drug prevention.
1987	Mrs. Reagan found out she had breast cancer.
1989	Mrs. Reagan started the Nancy Reagan Foundation.
1991	The Reagans opened the Ronald Reagan Presidential Library.
1994	Mr. Reagan was diagnosed with Alzheimer's disease.
2004	Mr. Reagan died on June 5.

Did You Know?

Nancy acted with famous Broadway star Mary Martin in *Lute Song*.

Mrs. Reagan starred in the film *Hellcats of the Navy* with her husband in 1956. The U.S. Navy used Hellcat fighter airplanes during World War II.

As California's First Lady, Mrs. Reagan wrote a newspaper column. She donated her salary to an organization that helps families of men and women who fought in the Vietnam War.

In 1981, Mrs. Reagan was honored to attend the royal wedding of Prince Charles and Princess Diana in England.

Mrs. Reagan's favorite color is red.

Mrs. Reagan's nickname for her husband was Ronnie.

Mrs. Reagan's "just say no" phrase became a popular slogan of the 1980s. Some elementary school antidrug programs still use it today.

Mrs. Reagan was awarded the Congressional Gold Medal of Honor in 2000 and the Presidential Medal of Freedom in 2002. Both awards recognized her lifelong volunteer work.

Glossary

Alzheimer's disease - an illness that causes forgetfulness, confusion, and overall mental disintegration.

assassinate - to murder a very important person, usually for political reasons.

astrologer - a person who studies how the positions of stars and planets supposedly influence human lives and events.

audition - to give a trial performance showcasing personal talent as a musician, a singer, a dancer, or an actor.

breast cancer - a disease characterized by an abnormal growth of cells in a person's breast that destroys healthy tissues and organs.

neurosurgeon - a doctor who performs operations on the nerves, the brain, or the spinal cord of a patient.

recession - a time when business activity slows.

Vietnam War - from 1957 to 1975. A long, failed attempt by the United States to stop North Vietnam from taking over South Vietnam.

World War II - from 1939 to 1945, fought in Europe, Asia, and Africa. Great Britain, France, the United States, the Soviet Union, and their allies were on one side. Germany, Italy, Japan, and their allies were on the other side.

Web Sites

To learn more about Nancy Reagan, visit ABDO Publishing Company on the World Wide Web at **www.abdopublishing.com**. Web sites about Nancy Reagan are featured on our Book Links page. These links are routinely monitored and updated to provide the most current information available.

Index